Asking Things Into Existence

How to query things into existence

Uncommon Results Book 2

FRANCIS JONAH

IMPORTANT

My name is Francis Jonah. I believe all things are possible. It is because of this belief that I have achieved so much in life. This belief extends to all. I believe every human being is equipped to succeed in every circumstance, regardless of the circumstance.

I know the only gap that exists between you and what you need to achieve or overcome is knowledge.

People are destroyed for lack of knowledge.

It is for this reason that I write short practical books that are so simple, people begin to experience immediate results as evidenced by the many testimonies I receive on a daily basis for my various books.

This book is no exception. You will obtain results because of it.

All scriptures are taken from the King James Version of the Bible unless otherwise stated.

Visit my website for powerful articles and materials

www.francisjonah.com

FREE GIFT

Just to say Thank You for downloading my book,
I'd like to give you these books for free.

Get these 4 powerful books today for free and
give yourself a great future.

Send me an email to get them

drfrancisjonah@gmail.com

Your testimonies will abound. You can look for my other books. They have produced many testimonies and I want your testimony to be one too.

Counselling Or Prayer

Send me an email if you need prayer or counsel or you have a question.

Better still if you want to make my acquaintance

My email is drfrancisjonah@gmail.com

Other books by Francis Jonah

1. 3 Day Fasting Challenge: How to receive manifestation of answers

2. How to Have Outrageous Financial Abundance In No Time:Biblical Principles For Immediate And Overwhelming Financial Success

3. 5 Bible Promises, Prayers and Decrees That Will Give You The Best Year Ever: A book for Shaping Every Year Successfully plus devotional (Book Of Promises 1)

4. Influencing The Unseen Realm: How to Influence The Spirit Realm for Victory in The Physical Realm(Spiritual Success Books)

5. Prayer That Works: Taking Responsibility For Answered Prayer

6. Healing The Sick In Five Minutes:How Anyone Can Heal Any Sickness

7. The Financial Miracle Prayer

8. The Best Secret To Answered Prayer

9. The Believer's Authority(Authority Of The Believer,Power And Authority Of The Believer)

10. The Healing Miracle Prayer

11. I Shall Not Die: Secrets To Long Life And
    Overcoming The Fear of Death

12. Three Straightforward Steps To Outrageous
    Financial Abundance: Personal Finance (Finance
    Made Easy Book 1)

13. Prayers For Financial Miracles: And 3 Ways To
    Receive Answers Quickly

14. Book: 3 Point Blueprint For Building Strong
    Faith: Spiritual:Religious:Christian:Motivational

15. How To Stop Sinning Effortlessly

16. The Power Of Faith-Filled Words

17. All Sin Is Paid For: An Eye Opening Book

18. Be Happy Now:No More Depression

19. The Ultimate Christian: How To Win In Every Life Situation: A book full of Revelations

20. Books:How To Be Free From Sicknesses And Diseases(Divine Health): Divine Health Scriptures

21. Multiply Your Personal Income In Less Than 30 Days

22. Ultimate Method To Memorize The Bible Quickly: (How To Learn Scripture Memorization)

23. Overcoming Emotional Abuse

24. Passing Exams The Easy Way: 90% and above in exams (Learning Simplified)

25. Books:Goal Setting For Those In A Hurry To Achieve Fast

26. Do Something Lest You Do Nothing

27. Financial Freedom:My Personal Blue-Print Made Easy For Men And Women

28. Why Men Go To Hell

29. Budgeting Tools And How My Budget Makes Me More Money

30. How To Raise Capital In 72 Hours: Quickly and Effectively Raise Capital Easily in Unconventional Ways (Finance Made Easy)

31. How To Love Unconditionally

32. Financial Independence: The Simple Path I Used To Wealth

33. Finding Happiness: The Story Of John Miller: A Christian Fiction

34. Finance Made Easy (2 Book Series)

Click here to see my author page

Contents

INTRODUCTION

CHAPTER ONE

CHAPTER TWO

CHAPTER THREE

CHAPTER FOUR

CHAPTER FIVE

CHAPTER SIX

CHAPTER SEVEN

CHAPTER EIGHT

CHAPTER NINE

CHAPTER TEN

INTRODUCTION

Questions are a powerful tool in the hands of the believer? Even God used questions to accomplish one purpose or the other.

The evidence of God asking questions is all over the Bible:

He asked Adam, "Where are you?"

He asked Jonah, "Why are you angry?"

He asked satan, "Have you considered my servant Job?"

He asked Moses, "What is in your hand?"

He asked Ezekiel, "Can these dry bones live?"

The list goes on and on, and for every question that God asked, the purpose was different.

He had a specific use for each question.

Questions are tools we can use to seek and find certain answers in life.

The scripture below typifies the ability to use questions to get certain results:

Mat 7:7 Ask, and it shall be given you; seek, and ye shall find; knock, and it shall be opened unto you:

Mat 7:8 For every one that asketh receiveth; and he that seeketh findeth; and to him that knocketh it shall be opened.

Matthew 7:7-8

Everyone that asks receives. We can use questions to ask for things and receive them.

Everyone that seeks finds. We can use questions to seek things and we shall find them.

Questions can be used to knock on certain doors and they shall be opened.

Imagine asking "Is John around?" in front of John's house. It is likely the door will be opened for you.

Questions play significant roles in making things come to pass and the ability to ask the right questions is a valuable skill that every believer needs to learn and use. The scriptures are clear on that much. When you seek, you will find.

Some people ask the wrong questions and thus receive answers that lead them nowhere. Their lives become a heap of frustration just because of the questions they asked.

Others ask the right questions and are released into a world of great possibilities. Possibilities that wouldn't have been so had it not been for the right questions they asked.

There are things you want to come to pass in your life? You want to see them manifest in your life but you do not know how to go about it.

This is where questions come in, they help you access what is available and prepared for you to possess.

Prosperity, power, healing, favour, anointing, grace, increase, promotion and enlargement are available. To know how to access them and enjoy them, you need to ask questions, not just any questions, you need to ask the right questions that will deliver the manifestation to you.

You will learn how to access what is available to you using Biblical questions, methods and principles.

Two basic things will be spoken about in this book, how to ask things into existence and how to query or question things into existence. They all stem from one Biblical principle of asking.

The foundations of the book will be laid up to chapter four. The operational principles take effect from chapter five. I will however urge you to read chapter by chapter so that you can get the full benefit of the book.

Get ready to be overwhelmed with the manifestation of answers in your life as you learn how to ask things into existence.

Books In The Uncommon Results Series:

Book 1: Speaking Things Into Existence

Book 2: Asking Things Into Existence

Book 3: Praying Things Into Existence

CHAPTER ONE:

USES OF QUESTIONS

Questions have several uses. Knowing the various ways to use questions will help you, the believer, maximize their use and profit considerably from them.

Among the uses of questions are:

1. To elicit answers that provide useful information

2. To start conversations

3. To involve people and retain interest

4. To help people think and discover things

5. To help self-introspection

Although there are many uses of questions, at the end of the day we will focus on the use of questions to discover things and to gain useful information. For now, let us delve deeper into all the aforementioned uses so that we can use questions well in our lives.

To elicit answers that provide useful information

Questions help us to elicit answers that provide useful information. We need information for most of the things we do and the easiest way to get this information is to ask questions.

When Jesus wanted to know where they could find bread to feed the multitudes who gathered to hear him, he asked a question.

Joh 6:5 When Jesus then lifted up his eyes, and saw a great company come unto him, he saith unto Philip, Whence shall we buy bread, that these may eat?

John 6:5

That question provided him with the useful information that there were 5 loaves of bread and two fish available.

With that information, he was able to perform one of the most incredible miracles of history.

He fed over 5000 people;

Joh 6:9 There is a lad here, which hath five barley loaves, and two small fishes: but what are they among so many?

Joh 6:10 And Jesus said, Make the men sit down. Now there was much grass in the place. So the men sat down, in number about five thousand.

Joh 6:11 And Jesus took the loaves; and when he had given thanks, he distributed to the disciples, and the disciples to them that were set down; and likewise of the fishes as much as they would.

Joh 6:12 When they were filled, he said unto his disciples, Gather up the fragments that remain, that nothing be lost.

John 6:9-12

Questions elicit answers that provide useful information.

If you use questions and get into the word of God primarily as well as other sources for answers, you will get useful information to guide you.

When you need useful information, remember to ask questions.

To start conversations

Another use of question is to start conversations.

Man is a relational being. This means that, we have the need to relate with other human beings. One way to relate is to have conversations with others and a great way to start conversations is to ask questions.

A simple "How are you?" or "Can you direct me to the bus top?" or even "May I know your name?" can easily help you start conversations with others.

You can even start conversations with God using questions. They are great conversation starters granted you are sensitive to Him and are using the right questions.

When Jesus wanted to have a conversation with the Samaritan woman, he asked her a question. That question started a conversation that led to the whole town hearing about the messiah.

Joh 4:7 When a Samaritan woman came to draw water, Jesus said to her, "Will you give me a drink?"

John 4:7 NIV

This simple question, *"will you give me a drink?"* led to a conversation that has been studied as an evangelism classic.

Conversations can be started with God and His word. Yes, the word of God can also have conversations. You can do that using questions.

If you want to start conversations, just use questions.

To involve people and retain interest

You can use questions to involve people in what you are engaged in. You can also retain the interest of people you are teaching or engaged in conversation with using questions.

People easily get bored when they are not involved. For this reason, you can use questions to solicit their response or get them involved.

Jesus always taught his disciples, but sometimes, to get them involved, he would ask them questions. On one such occasion, he asked them a question and had one of the greatest involvements of their time together.

Mat 16:13 When Jesus came into the coasts of Caesarea Philippi, he asked his disciples, saying, Whom do men say that I the Son of man am?

Mat 16:14 And they said, Some say that thou art John the Baptist: some, Elias; and others, Jeremias, or one of the prophets.

Mat 16:15 He saith unto them, But whom say ye that I am?

Mat 16:16 And Simon Peter answered and said, Thou art the Christ, the Son of the living God.

Mat 16:17 And Jesus answered and said unto him, Blessed art thou, Simon Barjona: for flesh and blood hath not revealed it unto thee, but my Father which is in heaven.

Mat 16:18 And I say also unto thee, That thou art Peter, and upon this rock I will build my church; and the gates of hell shall not prevail against it.

Matthew 16:13-18

The question Jesus asked led to Peter making the powerful declaration about the sonship of Jesus. He pronounced Jesus the son of the living God.

Questions allow involvement and engagement, learn to use them for this purpose.

In matter of the Bible, if you use questions as you study the word of God, the word of God will also engage you and be involved in what you are doing.

To help people think and discover things

Another use of questions is to help people to think and discover things for themselves. Most discoveries in life are made with the help of questions.

Questions are also the medium that engage the mind the most to perform and bring results.

When a prophet was needed in Israel to clarify the word of God, the King of Judah, Jehoshaphat asked a question that led to the discovery of Elisha.

2Ki 3:11 But Jehoshaphat said, Is there not here a prophet of the LORD, that we may enquire of the LORD by him? And one of the king of Israel's servants answered and said, Here is Elisha the son of Shaphat, which poured water on the hands of Elijah.

2 Kings 3:11

Had that question not been asked, Elisha would not have been discovered by the Kings in question.

Is there something you have not discovered simply because you have not asked the right question?

Has your mind become dull and not engaged in solution thinking just because you are not asking questions?

Well, it is time to turn the corner. Ask questions.

To help self-introspection

Questions help the process of self-introspection. Sometimes we do not know how far we have veered of the reasonable path until we are presented with certain questions that aid self-introspection and repentance.

When Jonah was angry with God for making a plant die off, God asked him a question that made Jonah enter into a process of self-introspection.

Jon 4:9 And God said to Jonah, Doest thou well to be angry for the gourd? And he said, I do well to be angry, even unto death.

Jon 4:10 Then said the LORD, Thou hast had pity on the gourd, for the which thou hast not laboured, neither madest it grow; which came up in a night, and perished in a night:

Jon 4:11 And should not I spare Nineveh, that great city, wherein are more than sixscore thousand persons that cannot discern between their right hand and their left hand; and also much cattle?

Jonah 4:9-11

One day a man claims he asked himself this question or rather the question came to him, "if this was your son, would you do that to him?" This question came to him at a time he wanted to cheat a young man out of his inheritance.

That question helped him self introspect and correct his agenda against the young man.

If you want proper self-introspection, learn to ask questions.

The next chapter explains how questions lead to certain results in life and how to ask the right questions as a result?

CHAPTER TWO:

QUESTIONS DIRECT YOU TO PARTICULAR ANSWERS

We are all looking to have certain things manifest in our lives. For some, it is health, for others it is love and marriage, for others it is financial prosperity. The list is endless.

You may have your own list of things you would want manifested. Everyone does.

However, there is one certainty, and that is, no matter what you want to bring into existence in your life, questions can direct you to that point of manifestation.

In this chapter, we will study some major question types and how you can to use them to receive answers in your life.

These answers you will receive are the keys to whatever you want to bring into existence in your life. I am enjoying the journey of asking already.

The possibilities when you explore that realm are endless.

For the purpose of this book, we will not study all types of questions. We will only study the ones relevant to our aim of asking things into existence.

Thus, the questions we will look at are:

1. How

2. Who

3. When

4. Where

5. Why

6. What

7. Which

With these questions, we are believing God to formulate the basis for which you can ask certain questions that will get you exactly what you are looking for in life.

Our needs are many and may vary but the explanations that will come will simplify things for all to know how to ask and get the answers needed for manifestation in their individual lives.

Let us now proceed to talk about each type of question we will be using to query things into existence.

How

Questions with how are very significant. They bring about the highest number of results for people.

At least, I know they have blessed me the most. More than any other type of question.

"How" questions speak mostly to methodology. When you want something accomplished and you do not know the methodology to use to accomplish it, you normally employ the "how" question.

This question was employed in the Bible on several occasions to get the methodology for certain things to happen.

A popular occasion the "How" question was used is when Mary wanted to know the methodology by which a virgin could give birth.

Luk 1:34 Then said Mary unto the angel, How shall this be, seeing I know not a man?

Luke 1:34

This question got the appropriate answer and truly, the virgin was able to conceive.

Luk 1:35 And the angel answered and said unto her, The Holy Ghost shall come upon thee, and the power of the Highest shall overshadow thee: therefore also that holy thing which shall be born of thee shall be called the Son of God.

Luke 1:35

The same way that Mary got an answer from the "How" question she asked, that caused the manifestation and birth of Jesus Christ, your "How" questions will also bring about such answer to cause manifestation in your life.

Do not be afraid to ask "How" when you need certain things to manifest in your life.

Even though we will go deeper to learn how to ask questions and what to do after you ask them, understand that whatever you want to manifest, a "How" question can give you the methodology you need.

Examples of "How" questions are:

How long should I pray to receive answers?

How do I manifest the blessing of God?

How do I make my faith strong?

How do I multiply my finances?

These questions will lead you on a quest for answers. These answers will absolutely transform your life once you find the right ones. They will cause a harvest of manifestations.

Now that we have seen examples of the "How" question, let us move on to the "Who" question.

Who

The who question is a very relevant question. This is because it directs you to a person.

"Who" questions refer mostly to people or personalities.

When you want something accomplished and want to know who can get it done, the "Who" question can be employed.

It can also be employed if you want to know the person responsible for something.

This type of question was also employed in the Bible a couple of times. This is one occasion:

Luk 8:45 And Jesus said, Who touched me? When all denied, Peter and they that were with him said, Master, the multitude throng thee and press thee, and sayest thou, Who touched me?

Luke 8:45

Jesus asked this question because someone had drawn virtue out of him. Sure enough, because of the question, the woman responsible for touching him came out and was identified.

"Who" questions will help you determine the person responsible for certain things.

Imagine someone does not know the person who has the name which is above all names.

The "Who" question will lead that person to Jesus, who has the name above every name. At its mention, all knees bow and all tongues confess that Jesus is Lord.

How to use the "Who" question to help you make things manifest will be shared in later chapters.

This chapter is just to introduce you to the types of questions.

Some examples of "Who" questions are as follows:

Who controls the results of the words I speak?

Who is responsible for changing my mind?

Who saved me from my sins?

Who determines my failure in life?

These "Who" questions will lead you to important people who can help you manifest your desires.

Now that we have seen some examples of "Who" questions, let us proceed to learn about "When" questions.

When

The "when" question speaks to period. It helps determine the period of an event or manifestation.

It is important so that one can know whether something has happened or is about to happen or is happening.

There are many instances the "When" question is employed in the Bible.

Among them is the time David used it to express his hunger for God, which was so massive.

The "When" question will help you determine the period for the manifestation of whatever you want to see.

It can specifically tell you that 3 days is what you need to see certain results. The "When" question gives confidence and actually provides you with something to look up to.

In other instances, it helps you know things God has done already or is about to do. In the Bible, there are so many things God has already done but believers are not aware because they have not asked the "When" question.

One example of a "When" question is in the book of Psalms:

Psa 42:2 My soul thirsteth for God, for the living God: when shall I come and appear before God?

Psalm 42:2

David wanted to know when He could experience God. In the same chapter he receives a timing for His experience of the loving kindness of God.

Psa 42:8 Yet the LORD will command his lovingkindness in the daytime, and in the night his song shall be with me, and my prayer unto the God of my life.

Psalm 42:8

"When" questions will lead you to periods, you will be able to determine whatever periods you need for manifestation by asking the right "When" question.

Some crucial questions in this direction include:

When do I fast for maximum results?

When is the best time to give?

When will God bless me?

When will I overcome my challenges?

The when question will set many people free and give them hope as well as faith to pursue their desires.

Now that we have examples of "When" questions, let us move on to "Where" questions.

Where

"Where" questions speak to location.

If you want to find the location of something, it is appropriate you ask a "Where" question.

"Where" questions also talk about people something is with.

For instance, if you have a watch and you ask where it is, you can be told it is with someone. That person will lead you to the location of your watch.

Finally, the "Where" question can be used when you want someone to demonstrate their presence. Be it in terms of speaking or performing one action or the other.

The "Where" question is used many times in the Bible.

One of such occasions it is used is when Elisha asked for the God of Elijah.

Clearly, He wanted the God of Elijah to demonstrate His presence.

2Ki 2:14 And he took the mantle of Elijah that fell from him, and smote the waters, and said, Where is the LORD God of Elijah? and when he also had smitten the waters, they parted hither and thither: and Elisha went over.

2 Kings 2:14

After that question, God demonstrated His presence and power by parting the waters of the Jordan.

"Where" questions will lead you to locations, people with things you need and the demonstration of presence.

You can see why it is a very important question to cause manifestation. People can easily show their presence when that question is asked.

Some crucial questions in that direction include:

Where is the power of God today?

Where can I find peace?

Where do I go for salvation?

Where can I go to be taught well as a believer?

Now that we have seen examples of "Where" questions, let us move on to "Why" questions.

Why

Why questions speak to reason. They find out the reason for things.

Sometimes a good reason is all you need to go all out and do something great.

That is what this type of question gives you. A good reason.

In the Bible, there are so many "Why" questions. One of the "Why" questions is seen when Jesus wanted to know the reason the disciples slept during prayer.

Luk 22:46 And said unto them, Why sleep ye? rise and pray, lest ye enter into temptation.

Luke 22:46

That question was answered for us. It was sorrow that had caused them to sleep instead of to pray. That was the reason for their sleeping.

Luk 22:45 And when he rose up from prayer, and was come to his disciples, he found them sleeping for sorrow,

Luke 22:45

"Why" questions are relevant because they give important reasons. These reasons may be the only fuel you have to do something significant.

These reasons can also give you ideas about how to solve the root cause of certain issues

Do not be hesitant to ask such questions.

Examples of why questions are:

Why do we pray?

Why do we give?

Why do we fast?

Why do we work?

"Why" questions are powerful questions. There are things people will never do unless they get a good "Why". Finding such reasons is a key to many doors.

Now that we have seen some examples of "Why" questions, let us move on to "What" questions.

What

"What" questions speak to items, methods, principles, reasons and many more.

They deal with a variety if things based on how they are used.

They also bring about a whole range of answers that are beneficial to the one that asks the question.

Used well, a whole lot of information can be acquired. Information that can be transformational in nature.

This type of question is used several times in the Bible. One of such times is when the prison warden wanted to know what he must do to be saved:

Act 16:27 And the keeper of the prison awaking out of his sleep, and seeing the prison doors open, he drew out his sword, and would have killed himself, supposing that the prisoners had been fled.

Act 16:28 But Paul cried with a loud voice, saying, Do thyself no harm: for we are all here.

Act 16:29 Then he called for a light, and sprang in, and came trembling, and fell down before Paul and Silas,

Act 16:30 And brought them out, and said, Sirs, what must I do to be saved?

Acts16:27-30

Based on the question he asked, he received the answer that brought about his salvation.

Your next question can also bring you salvation or deliverance.

Examples of "What" questions are:

What can I do to have strong faith?

What can I do to increase my finances?

What is the cure for prayerlessness?

What makes people angry?

Now that you have seen examples of "What" questions, let us proceed to the last type of question for the purposes of this book.

Which

"Which" questions speak to several things.

They speak to people, places, reasons, truths and methods.

They can be applied in a variety of ways to get answers that are relevant to manifestation of things you desire.

They are also used in the Bible several times. A typical example of when it was used is when a lawyer asked Jesus for the greatest commandment.

Mat 22:36 Master, which is the great commandment in the law?

Matthew 22:36

Sure enough, Jesus answered his question and the truth was revealed to him.

Interestingly, Jesus answered more than necessary.

Mat 22:37 Jesus said unto him, Thou shalt love the Lord thy God with all thy heart, and with all thy soul, and with all thy mind.

Mat 22:38 This is the first and great commandment.

Mat 22:39 And the second is like unto it, Thou shalt love thy neighbour as thyself.

Matthew 22:37-39

The "Which" question is an important question that can help you bring about manifestation.

Examples include:

Which spiritual law can make me rich?

Which prayer can resolve my problems?

Which scripture can help me develop patience?

Which book of the Bible will help me with righteousness?

Now that you know how questions can direct you to important answers that can help you reach the goals you want in life and the manifestations you want to see; we can move to the next chapter.

We are moving on to study the wrong kind of questions that bring little or no profit to us, so that we can avoid them as much as possible.

This will be the foundation upon which we can now learn the questions to ask that will bring things into existence in our lives.

CHAPTER THREE:

AVOIDING WRONG QUESTIONS

When we speak about wrong questions in this chapter, we are not talking about your typical wrong question. We are talking about questions that seem to do less for those who ask them.

It is to say that these questions do not lead us to the kind of manifestations that we are looking for.

We want questions that can help us bring certain things like increase and promotion into existence in our lives.

If the questions we ask are not in alignment with these goals, then for our purposes, it is the wrong kind of question.

Also, for our purposes, wrong questions can be questions that actually stem from a wrong mindset.

Hopefully, every wrong mindset will be corrected as you go through this chapter.

With the proper mindset, proper and correct questions can be asked which will lead to the answers that will draw you closer to what you want in life.

Let us examine the type of questions we deem wrong in our quest to query things into existence.

1. Questions for general knowledge

2. Questions of blame

3. Victim mentality questions

4. Questions that cause wars after the flesh

5. Witchcraft Questions

We will take each question and explain it so that you can avoid them when seeking manifestation in your life.

Questions for General Knowledge

In our quest to pose the right questions to receive the kind of manifestation in our lives, we must not engage so much in general knowledge questions.

Some people spend their time looking for the age of the oldest person in the Bible and his name.

Although such information is good for the purpose of general knowledge, it will hardly lead to any revelation that will make impact in your life.

Some people make it a habit of arguing over such issues that contribute little to their lives.

That should not be you. You are in pursuit of higher value knowledge.

Listen to this story:

There was a man who was very sick in his body. Although he was sick, he was searching through scriptures in his Bible and also on the internet.

A very commendable act.

Curious to know what was going on, his favourite neighbour asked him what he was doing.

To this question he replied that he was looking for the names of the siblings of Jesus Christ.

Beloved, there is nothing wrong with knowing the names of the siblings of Jesus Christ. However, you would think that for a man who was sick, he would be looking for information in the Bible and in books as to how he can receive healing.

No, he was more interested in a general knowledge question and not a manifestation question.

Those are the kind of questions we mean by general knowledge questions. "Who were the siblings of Jesus?" kind of questions.

Please avoid them when there are pressing needs to be met. You can go to them when you have met your major needs.

Questions of blame

There is another type of question we must avoid else our manifestations will never happen.

These are questions of blame. Typical examples of such questions include:

Why doesn't God answer my prayer?

Why is God delaying my healing?

Why did God make me lose so much money?

In all these questions, it seems to me that people are blaming God for things they should be responsible for.

Contrary to what these questions suggest, the Bible suggests differently.

God does answer prayers, there are so many testimonies of that.

It is some people who do not know how to receive answers to their prayer. Yet these group of people would not ask the right questions to get the right knowledge. They will conveniently keep blaming God and they will also keep doing whatever they were doing in the past that was not bringing them results in prayer.

God does heal, evidence of it is all over in the Bible. There are also living men and women who can testify of being healed by God.

Because God is not partial, he doesn't heal some people and leave others, if there is anyone to blame when one does not receive healing, it shouldn't be God.

We need to look at ourselves first and then we can take responsibility to get the results we need.

Instead of blaming God with our questions, a better question for healing could be, "who can I contact who is very anointed in healing to help me?" or "How do I get my healing, is there something I must do?"

These questions asked above do not blame God or anyone else, they actually help us get the solutions we need.

If we keep asking questions of blame, chances of getting solutions will be minimal.

Victim Mentality Questions

Victim mentality questions are the worst of the lot.

They are typically asked to show the helplessness of the one asking.

They are the questions that start with "why me God".

Beloved, there is no hopeless case with God and no one is a victim until they make themselves victims.

Many of the people who play the victim card are sadly responsible for most of the things they experience. Although there is a tiny minority who we cannot say so of, most people who try to behave as if they are victims of God or men are actually responsible for where they are.

Take a woman who is warned several times about a man she is dating; she ignores all warnings and advice and moves in with the man.

Years down the line, you will hear the "why me God, why did you allow me to go through all this?" question. Or better still you will hear "Why me God, why did you put this sickness on me?"

The truth of the matter is that, it is our choices that lead us into many of the troubles and predicaments we find ourselves in.

The best thing to do in such cases is to take responsibility and seek a way out. That is how to be free of any negative circumstances. The victim mentality doesn't help.

A better question than the why me is "How did I get here?", "How can I correct my ways?"

Let us move on to the next type of questions to avoid.

Questions that cause wars of the flesh

There are certain questions that cause fights and strife among brethren whiles the real enemy, the devil, is left Scott-free.

In a meeting one day, a lady who was in need of a child asked me such a question. 'Who is responsible for my not being able to give birth, I am sure it is one of my aunties"

She wanted me to say it was her auntie, so that she could start world war 3 with her.

Well, the devil is the one behind such issues or sometimes our own mistakes. Nonetheless, regardless of the devil or our mistakes, God is able to give us children.

What such questions do is that they cause people to start fighting relatives and what have you when the real enemy is relaxing and sipping orange juice.

I would never forget the story of some young women who ganged up to pray against their grandmother because, to them, she was responsible for their poverty in life.

Beloved, this grandmother of theirs died and they rejoiced greatly. To them, their poverty was over because the one responsible was dead.

Ten years down the line, I can confirm to you that none of them has prospered financially. They are still in the rank they used to be when their grandmother was alive.

We do not war after the flesh. Let us avoid questions that cause fleshly wars and strife among family members and brethren.

The real person we must fight is the devil and his host of agents.

The next type of questions is quite interesting, some may call it serious.

Witchcraft questions

Witchcraft questions are simply questions that seek to know how to do evil.

Some of these questions include, "how do I take her husband from her?"

"How do I make this man serve me like a dog?"

"Which medicine can I use so that this woman never leaves me?"

"What can I do so that he forgets his children?"

Beloved, such questions are evil and are not worthy of believers.

It is venturing into witchcraft, and God frowns mightily upon it.

It is my prayer that we would never venture into that area of questions.

Now that we have a good foundation of the kind of questions that stem from a wrong mindset and should be avoided as much as possible, we are ready to enter the real meat of the message of the book "Asking Things into Existence".

If you are ready to learn, turn to the next chapter and let us delve deeper.

CHAPTER FOUR:

POWER OF QUESTIONS

Questions are very powerful. In this chapter, we are going to discover the reasons why questions are that powerful and why we must use them in our quest to see manifestations in our lives.

Nothing happens for happening sake and in order for believers to walk in the things God has made available to them, they need to cooperate with God.

Take the scenario below, I believe it will help you understand what I mean by cooperating with God.

If you have a daughter who is a teenager and that child is sick and you bring medicine to her to take for her health and healing, you expect that child to cooperate with you by taking the medicine so that the sickness will go.

If your teenage daughter tells you she will take the medicine, but doesn't take it, she will continue to be sick.

The reason she will continue being sick is not that there was no medicine available for her healing but the fact that she refused to cooperate with you by not taking the medicine.

Because believers have their own free will and can choose to do what they like, it is their choice to cooperate with God in order to enjoy the things He has made available to them.

This scripture makes us understand the power of our choices and why it is up to us to cooperate with God:

Deu 30:19 I call heaven and earth to record this day against you, that I have set before you life and

death, blessing and cursing: therefore choose life,
that both thou and thy seed may live:

Deuteronomy 30:19

This is powerful, God encourages us to choose life, although we can choose death, He encourages us to choose life. At the end of the day, it is our choice.

It is interesting how it says we can choose death or cursing. You would think nobody will make that choice, but many of us do that all the time through our words, our mindsets and our actions.

That is why we must learn to take responsibility for our progress in life.

Let us now look at the power of questions. Among the powers that questions possess are the following:

1. Questions have the power to keep the mind working even when we are unaware.

2. Questions have the power to change our perspectives

3. Questions have the power to help us take action

4. Questions have the power to remove limits from our lives

Now that we have discovered these powers that questions possess, let us go down and explain them better so we can use them to our benefit.

Let us start with the first one:

Questions have the power to keep the mind working even when we are unaware

The believer is supposed to take full advantage of his body, soul and spirit to further his cause here on earth.

When all these dimensions of man are not used fully, there is an imbalance somewhere and the prosperity and excellence of the believer becomes somewhat lacking.

Many believers fall victim to not using all their three dimensions properly. Most especially, they do not engage their souls(minds) properly.

The predominant time most believers engage their minds is when they are worrying. This is a negative and wrong use of the mind and this truth was echoed by Jesus himself when he asked:

Can any one of you by worrying add a single hour to your life?

Matthew 6:27 NIV

Since worrying has no benefit to the believer, there needs to be a better engagement of the mind. An engagement of the mind that is geared towards progress and this is where questions come in.

The mind is a unique tool designed by God in such a way that when it is engaged, even when you are not conscious of it, it is still working on that which you have engaged it. Even in our sleep, our minds continue to work on the assignments we have given it.

That is how powerful the mind is. It is a workaholic that is only satisfied after it accomplishes the tasks assigned to it.

This is good news for everyone who knows how to engage the mind positively.

This is because even if you are unaware, the mind will work over time to bring the solution you need.

How do you then engage the mind to bring you the answers you seek? It is simple.

By asking good questions, you activate the mind to work and bring you answers.

Is your problem a health problem or a financial problem? Once you engage the mind with the right questions, it will certainly bring you a solution.

The solution may come in a few minutes or a few months, but one thing is sure, the mind will definitely bring out the answer.

Many times, when I write and there is an example I am looking for in the Bible, once I ask the question (e.g. where did God deliver someone from death?), sometimes within minutes my mind brings out the information I need.

At other times it doesn't come immediately but as I have conversations with other people, they say certain things and immediately my mind is triggered. It points out to me that; this is the answer to the question I asked.

So, you see, the mind is always working when you engage it, whether you are aware or not.

The mind is that powerful. To the extent that when you give it an assignment, even when you are unaware that it is working to find the answer, it is?

A simple question like "what can I do to prosper?" can send the mind on a solution spree and contact the solution for you through many mediums.

Either the messages you have listened to or are listening to, your Bible readings, the tv you watch, the billboards you see or even the conversation you have with people.

The mind is that powerful when it is engaged to find a solution. That engagement is done with questions.

It is my prayer that from today you will begin to engage your mind through good questions that will lead to lasting solutions for your life, ministry, career and family.

On to the next power questions possess.

Questions have the power to change our perspectives

Questions have the power to change our perspective about things.

Many of us are stuck in old ways of thinking. Even though we try to break those old thinking patterns, we keep doing it in a not so efficient manner.

Many of us use statements to try to break our old ways of thinking. Such thinking patterns may be difficult to break when statements are used.

Questions however have a subtle way of getting to people and causing their minds to do some deep thinking even with them not being aware of it.

This deep thinking on the subconscious level helps break old ways of thinking.

I remember I was asked a question one day.

For three days, that question kept ringing in my mind and causing my perspective to change on several issues.

I had resisted a change in opinion for so long, despite the many statements I had heard to change my opinion. That question was the game changer, it really broke me down.

Imagine trying your best to do little in the kingdom of God and then a subtle question is asked "is that the best you can do for God?".

Such a question has a way of entering the deep recesses of your soul and redirecting your perspectives about many things.

Many a time, when you seek to change the perspectives of people, do not force it with statements, try going with questions, it will change perspectives and mindsets faster. It may not be immediate and forceful, but it is an effective approach.

Regarding your own thinking patterns and mindsets that need to be changed, questions will do that faster for you.

Instead of statements like "improve your life?", a question like "is it possible to improve your life?" will be more effective and wonders for you.

Questions possess that much power and the earlier we realise it and begin to use it to our advantage, the better life will be for us.

Questions have the power to help us take action

Questions have the power to help us take action. Taking action is one of the greatest hallmarks of a believer. The Bible puts it in no uncertain terms:

Jas 1:22 But be ye doers of the word, and not hearers only, deceiving your own selves.

Jas 1:23 For if any be a hearer of the word, and not a doer, he is like unto a man beholding his natural face in a glass:

Jas 1:24 For he beholdeth himself, and goeth his way, and straightway forgetteth what manner of man he was.

Doing the word requires action and questions have the power to make us act.

Passivity is never encouraged in the kingdom. It is akin to laziness and that is why activity that brings positive results is always encouraged.

Typical questions that instigate action include, "what can I do today to make me a better Christian?"

This seemingly simple question can cause you to study the word of God, pray, fast, give or even go out on evangelism.

Questions are that powerful in helping people take action. Take those who get saved when the question of those who want to be saved is asked. You see people lifting their hands and coming to the altar to get saved just because a question was asked.

Imagine that question was not asked, would these actions be taken for salvation to occur? I do not think so.

If you have been inactive and do not know how to jumpstart your life in one area or the other, it is time to ask yourself certain questions.

These questions will help you come back on track as a doer, an action taker and a result-oriented person.

If you find yourself inactive and lazy for a while, just start asking any of these questions:

Can I read one verse of scripture today?

Can I pray for 5 minutes today?

Can I fast for 3 hours today?

You will be surprised the kind of actions these questions would lead to.

Questions have the power to remove limits from our lives

Questions have the power to remove limits from the lives of individuals.

There are certain questions that have the capability of removing limits immediately they are asked.

It is important to note that many of us are operating in life under self-imposed limits.

Many of us are unaware of the several self-limiting beliefs we are operating under.

Some of these limits we are operating under were inherited since childhood, others we picked up as the challenges of life took a hard hit on us.

It takes the asking of certain questions to actually help us identify and break these limits.

A typical question like "why can't I be the Governor of my state?" will reveal to you the kind of limitations that have been operation unconsciously in your life.

There are many of such questions that will help break certain limits in your life in different areas of living.

Why can't I pray for 3 hours daily?

Why can't I be a billionaire?

Why can't I raise the dead?

Will you be bold enough to ask those questions in order to break the limits that pertain to your life and progress?

I know you would.

We are now ready to delve deeper into the word of God and explore the principles in the word to help us query things into being. I am excited already and so should you be.

Up on till now, we had not really delved into the key principles to operate with.

We were building the proper foundations, which we have now done. With those foundations, we are ready to make serious inroads.

FREE COURSE "21 Days To Answered Prayer"

If you bought the paperback version, please email me with the title **Free $100 Course** and I will send the course to you.

Please remember to send the exact title for the email;

Free $100 Course.

CHAPTER FIVE:

SEEK AND YOU SHALL FIND

It is true that the words of Jesus in the book of Matthew 7:7-8 are one of the best kept secrets in the world.

The revelations in that scripture are deep and its ability to bring about prosperity in the life of any individual cannot be underestimated.

When I say prosperity, I mean to excel regardless of the area of endeavour one chooses. This scripture is potent enough to cause anyone to excel in their chosen field of endeavour.

Let us look at the words of the scripture as we endeavour to benefit fully from them:

Mat 7:7 Ask, and it shall be given you; seek, and ye shall find; knock, and it shall be opened unto you:

Mat 7:8 For every one that asketh receiveth; and he that seeketh findeth; and to him that knocketh it shall be opened.

Matthew 7:7-8

These words are deep and powerful. If you ask, you shall receive. This is a statement of truth. It is a spiritual principle and it works.

Same applies to seeking and finding and then knocking and the door being open.

These are the kind of principles that excite me in the word of God. They are sure formulas that work for anyone who will work them.

I am confident you will work these spiritual principles to the latter so that you can experience some serious results.

Because we can take God at His word, we can confidently explore the benefits of the scriptures He has made available to us.

Questions lead you to seek

If seeking makes you find, then the fastest way to embark on a seeking expedition is to ask a question.

It makes sense because a seeking expedition is equal to a finding expedition according to the Bible.

A question like "How do I heal the sick?" can take you on a journey of seeking. This seeking initiated by the question will cause you to find the relevant knowledge that will make you a great healer of the sick.

There is an assurance from the word of God that you will definitely find the keys that will make you heal the sick once you seek it.

Once the question triggers your seeking, the Bible says you will find it.

That is good news. One you are seeking; you can be guaranteed of one truth. The truth that you will find what you are looking for. If I sound overconfident, it is because of this:

Num 23:19 God is not a man, that he should lie; neither the son of man, that he should repent: hath he said, and shall he not do it? or hath he spoken, and shall he not make it good?

Numbers 23:19

Men lie. God doesn't.

Men are dishonest. God is honest.

Men are unfaithful. God is always faithful.

This means that, if a man doesn't find what he seeks, it simply means he wasn't seeking. Whoever seeks, finds.

This also makes sense because in every situation God must be true and every man a liar:

Rom 3:4 God forbid: yea, let God be true, but every man a liar; as it is written, That thou mightest be justified in thy sayings, and mightest overcome when thou art judged.

Romans 3:4

I buy into the truth that the man that doesn't find is not seeking because so many men spend five minutes in searching for things of great importance and they want to find it.

This is juxtaposed to other men using forty days to find that same thing.

Five minutes of seeking is not seeking, that is playing at best. When men seek treasures like gold and diamonds, they do not spend 5 minutes or an hour seeking.

They put in all their effort and time till they find what they seek. That is why I won't let the words of any man make me believe contrary to the word of God.

Very important

What many people call seeking is not seeking at all.

The time, effort and resources needed to find a dollar is not the same required to find a million dollars.

Many people are using the seeking formula for a dollar to seek for a million dollars. Brethren you will not find it.

The reason is simple, it takes more to seek and find a million dollars than it takes to seek and find a dollar.

Don't ever compare the two.

I know men who have gone on three years seeking journeys just to find what they were looking for and others who will not even use a month to seek.

Everything has a price, once you pay it, you have access to it.

Those who complain of seeking and not finding should save themselves the complains and understand this basic principle.

If you seek the way you are supposed to seek, you will find. If you just do anything pretending to seek, you will end up not finding.

And when you do not find, know that you have not put in what it takes to find.

There is nothing wrong with the principle. God is not mocked. You reap what you sow.

Gal 6:7 Be not deceived; God is not mocked: for whatsoever a man soweth, that shall he also reap.

Galatians 6:7

Those who seek, find.

Beloved, don't spend two hours looking for truth that will transform your entire life and the life of generations after you when that cannot even be qualified as a full day's work.

It is your life of over 20, 30,40 or 50 years we are talking about plus generations after you. That should be enough motivation to put in the time, effort and resources into seeking.

Questions cause you to seek and that is why they are important, the right questions will help you seek in the right direction, thus making it easier to find what you are looking for.

Once you find what you are looking for, manifestation follows.

That is why it is possible to query things into existence. The right question will lead you to how you can make what you want manifest.

No wonder the Bible says:

Joh 8:32 And ye shall know the truth, and the truth shall make you free.

John 8:32

The truth you know will bring you the freedom you seek in life. Seek truth first.

Whatever you don't find, you did not seek

Brethren, there is a mindset we must have in order to prosper on this earth. It is the mindset the word of God offers.

If the Bible says whatever you seek, you will find. It simply means that whatever you don't find, you did not seek.

It is as simple as that. This is the kind of mindset that will keep you going on to find that which you are looking for.

Do you know why you will keep on seeking? It is because deep within you, you know the answer exists. And the reason you know it exists is the new mindset you have cultivated based on the word of God.

I know it and you know it. The answer exists and many people are operating in that realm you want to operate in.

That alone is proof that the answer exists. People have found the key to prosperity because the sought it. Others have found the keys to divine healing because they sought it.

What will you also discover in your seeking?

Let me stray a little into something that happened in my life after I decided to use this key in my own unique way.

When I started as a writer, I had many complements and testimonies about how my books were transforming lives positively.

All over the world, I received such emails. I had a slight problem though; I was not selling as much books per day as I wanted.

I had a dream, call it a goal to sell 100 books minimum daily so that I could reach more people and impact their lives. At the time I was selling between 10 to 15 books day.

I began to seek how I could make that dream manifest.

For weeks I read many books, searched over 120 articles, watched over 30 videos, prayed and fasted. I did all these things for weeks.

This all paid off when I finally discovered the key I was looking for. In a matter of three months, 100 books a day had become so easy, I didn't even bother about whether I would sell 100 books a day or not. I always did.

The question "How do I sell 100 books a day?" led me to seek and to find the answer I was looking for.

Indeed, whatever you do not find, you did not seek. Guess what I am seeking now?

Your guess is as good as mine "How to sell 1000 books a day?"

This goal when accomplished will make the truth of the word of God that sets free and causes unimaginable success to reach more people.

That is what fills my heart with joy. Just yesterday I received an email from a brother and a call from a sister.

They were sharing powerful testimonies they had received a s a result of the teachings in my books. 1000 books a day is possible, if I don't find it, I did not seek it.

Currently, I am finding bits and pieces of knowledge that will take me there.

One thing is certain though, that knowledge is available and I would find it. What led me on that quest though is a simple question.

Is there a question you need to ask yourself concerning your finances, or your spiritual life or your relationship or your debt or your business?

Ask that question now, so that your seeking journey will begin.

You will find what you seek beloved. You will.

Those who seek find, not those who need

There are too many people needing and too few people seeking.

The scripture is quite clear:

Mat 7:8 For every one that asketh receiveth; and he that seeketh findeth; and to him that knocketh it shall be opened.

Matthew 7:8

It is those who seek that find, not those who need.

See if you can relate to this story.

A man of God visited a man who needed financial breakthrough. When he got to the man's house to pray for him and encourage him, the man had gathered 7 different movie series to watch on his TV.

Even though he was listening to the man of God, he did not even pause the series he was watching. His attention was divided.

The man of God wondered, he, the man of God did not have a financial problem but had read 3 books that month on financial breakthrough and searched for prayer keys that led to financial breakthrough so he could help this man.

The one with the problem though could not be bothered. He needed a financial breakthrough but he was not searching for it.

He was searching for entertainment in series.

Beloved, it is not those who need that find, it is those who seek. As we speak if there are things you need and you are not seeking to find, then there is a big issue somewhere.

You are on the wrong side of the principle in discussion and you need to align yourself quickly.

Those who seek find, not those who need. Bear that in mind. Stop needing and start seeking.

Where you seek

A very important variable in your journey of seeking is where you seek.

There are certain places, no matter how much time and energy you spend, you will never find gold.

It doesn't exist in those geographies. There are other places you will never find oil.

That is why in your quest to seek, you must seek in the right places. Don't go and ask a poor man the principles for wealth creation, neither should you go to where drunkards are to learn how to break negative addictions.

Many people are not finding what they are looking for because they are either not seeking at all or they are seeking in the wrong place.

Five gentlemen came to me seeking the keys to financial prosperity. Within three months, they had prospered greatly. They then revealed to me that they had been to several other places but couldn't find the keys to prosper like they did when they came to me.

The long and short of it is that, where you seek is important if you will find what you seek or not.

They had been to many places and not found the keys to prosperity. They could have complained that they have sought and didn't find, but they knew the principle was true and kept seeking till the found me.

I revealed the keys to them and they prospered.

How to seek

Seeking is somewhat easy to do in my opinion, although it is also difficult at the same time.

You seek by reading the Bible, listening to messages, watching videos and reading articles on the subject that you seek manifestation.

You can also seek by talking to mentors and knowledgeable pastors and men of God or successful people in certain endeavours.

You seek by asking relevant questions.

Knowledge is not automatic. You need to reach out to knowledgeable men of God with results to prove their knowledge and sound Biblical principles to back it.

You also back up your searching with a lot of prayer, fasting and meditation in the word of God. This speeds up your seeking process by a multiple of 100. It is a guaranteed truth.

It means that, if your original speed was 30, it becomes 3000 now. Yea, fasting and prayer are that powerful.

Seeking is as easy as that but requires a lot of effort and time to know which information is right and which one is wrong until you come to that which just works perfectly for you.

That is when you can apply and see the manifestation you desire. Let us go deeper in the next chapter. Before then;

My desire is to see your progress and prosperity and freedom from negative people and circumstances. Because of that, please permit me to introduce two courses that I believe passionately will help you.

1. To cure prayerlessness, an inconsistent prayer life and the pain of not enjoying all that God has made available to you,, click here to learn more about my 3 Day Course on "How to Overcome prayerlessness" that will solve the problem of prayerlessness in your life.

2.To overcome the pain of not having enough money to live where you want, eat what you want to eat and be a blessing to the multitudes around you, I have created a 7 Day Financial Abundance Course that will deliver financial abundance to you quickly.

Click here to learn more about that course.

You will see increase and enlargement as you step out in faith.

CHAPTER SIX: ASK AND YOU SHALL RECEIVE

Is there a sweeter promise or principle than this?

Just ask and you shall receive. This is what the word of God says. It is not the word of man to be doubted. It is the word of God to be believed.

Mat 7:7 Ask, and it shall be given you; seek, and ye shall find; knock, and it shall be opened unto you:

Mat 7:8 For every one that asketh receiveth; and he that seeketh findeth; and to him that knocketh it shall be opened.

Matthew 7:7-8

This is another powerful spiritual law to be taken advantage of and you should have every intention to take advantage of it with everything you are and have.

There are a few guidelines to this law that I need to open your eyes to.

Whatever you need is out there

If the Bible clearly states that if you ask, it shall be given to you, then it means that whatever you need is out there.

That is a great mindset to start with.

Make up your mind that whatever you need in life is out there. It is available. Whether it is healing, a house, a way out of your debt, growth in ministry, a marriage partner or what have you.

Once your mind is made up that what you are looking for is out there, it makes it easier to spend your time and effort to get it.

You know you will not be disillusioned at the end of the day because if there is any certainty about the existence of what you want, you have that evidence in the word of God.

What is left now is for you to ask and then you will receive knowing fully well that it is available.

That is wonderful. A simple example to test our asking prowess is this "can I have a car to help me do the work of ministry?"

Even in asking, I believe you have realised that we are using questions. Questions are that great to aid manifestation.

To that question, yes, you can have a car for ministry. You need to ask for it and that is why you must read further to know the supporting principles to make you successful in asking.

Let us delve deeper into the asking and receiving as there are principles we need to lock down.

When you ask for a fish, you will not get a snake

Concerning asking God for things, Jesus made it clear that He gives us exactly what we want not something different that would hurt us.

God is too loving and caring to engage in such deception and evil. Read all the verses below, especially the latter ones;

Mat 7:8 For every one that asketh receiveth; and he that seeketh findeth; and to him that knocketh it shall be opened.

Mat 7:9 Or what man is there of you, whom if his son ask bread, will he give him a stone?

Mat 7:10 Or if he ask a fish, will he give him a serpent?

Mat 7:11 If ye then, being evil, know how to give good gifts unto your children, how much more shall your Father which is in heaven give good things to them that ask him?

Matthew 7:8-11

This is a beautiful verse of scripture. I could sleep with it for years.

God is a giver, if we ask, He gives. He is better than our earthly fathers. Even our earthly fathers always seek to give us good things and God is better than them. Far better, so you can imagine His capacity and desire to give.

If you ask for a house, God will not give you a box.

Settle that in your mind. It is important you do. Lest I forget, this principle does not apply to God alone.

He is not the only one you can ask; He has channels of blessing here on earth too that you can ask and you will receive.

Learn to ask

There are certain people who find it very difficult to ask for things.

This is a mindset that must be broken else you will not get the full benefits of your life here on earth.

As much as other people are supposed to benefit from you, you are also to benefit from others.

As much as you are in a higher place than others, other people are also in a higher place than you.

It takes humility to ask. Proud people do not ask. They are even too proud to ask from God in prayer.

That should not be you, and if it is you, do well to repent.

2Ch 7:14 If my people, which are called by my name, shall humble themselves, and pray, and seek my face, and turn from their wicked ways; then will I hear from heaven, and will forgive their sin, and will heal their land.

2 Chronicles 7:14

With all due respect, it is time to humble yourself and ask. Pride won't take you anywhere.

I won't lie, I have had problems asking ever since I was a child. Maybe my training led to that, but off late, I have been able to achieve much asking for the help of others.

Break that habit of not allowing those God has put around you from doping their God given assignments of helping you.

Even Jesus had helpers. Helpers who stretched far beyond even his immediate helpers, the disciples.

I have humbled myself and asked people for things. It made me vulnerable and reduced my pride but it was well worth it.

Jesus asked for water from the Samaritan woman. He was humble enough to do so:

Joh 4:7 There cometh a woman of Samaria to draw water: Jesus saith unto her, Give me to drink.

John 4:7

On another occasion, he asked Peter to push his boat further for him so he could preach:

Luk 5:3 And he entered into one of the ships, which was Simon's, and prayed him that he would thrust out a little from the land. And he sat down, and taught the people out of the ship.

Luke 5:3

This same Jesus asked for a donkey when entering into Jerusalem:

Luk 19:30 Saying, Go ye into the village over against you; in the which at your entering ye shall find a colt tied, whereon yet never man sat: loose him, and bring him hither.

Luk 19:31 And if any man ask you, Why do ye loose him? thus shall ye say unto him, Because the Lord hath need of him.

Luke 19:30-31

Remember that if you do not ask, you do not receive. It is a basic principle.

The Bible says we should ask. You are no exception, neither am I.

A very revealing true story

I remember a time I asked my email list to help launch my book into a certain rank on the amazon kindle store so that it could be a bestseller.

Many of the people on the email list gladly bought for themselves, bought for others and even spread the word on social media. If you are one of those who did, I love you and I am grateful that you have taken your God given assignment of helping my ministry seriously.

There was one man though who replied my email and insulted me. He further preached to me that if God wanted me to be a bestseller, God will do it himself and I did not have to ask anyone on my email list for help to accomplish that.

Beloved, the book I asked my email list to help me with became a bestseller. The people God had given me had pulled through for me. I could also wait for God to do it himself according to my religious brother.

It taught me a grace lesson. People have certain mindsets that have kept them back in life and will continue to imprison them if they do not renew their minds. I speak more about that in my book, The Power of a Transformed Mind.

If God puts people around you who can help you, why do you need to wait till He comes Himself to do that which He has made provision for through people.

Imagine Jesus waiting for God to provide him with a boat when he could easily ask Peter for the boat.

A word to the wise is enough.

Know who to ask

One problem I have realised with people who do not get results from the word of God is that, they sometimes fail to meditate on the word enough to get precise knowledge.

The truth that the word of God says ask and you shall be given doesn't mean ask just anybody.

Several years ago, a woman asked me for an amount of money so she could buy a house for herself. It was so much money and even though she had not earned the right to ask me for that kind of money, the truth of the matter was that I did not even have that kind of money to buy myself a house.

Let alone to buy for someone else. I could not help her. That notwithstanding, there were other people who could easily give her three houses. She just had to find the right person to ask the right thing. That could be a lot of work, but it is worth it.

At that point in time, I was not the one she should have asked.

When you are asking for something, know who to ask. There are people who have an abundance of what you need and others who are lacking in it.

If you ask one who is lacking in what you need, you will obviously not get it. That is why you must put in the effort to know who exactly is the right person to ask.

One day without anybody asking me, I gave out suits and shoes. I have so many of them yet no one comes to ask me for any.

I therefore decided to give them out to as many people as I could. Most of them were strangers.

There is someone also asking the wrong person for shoes and suits when the person may not have.

Here I am with shoes and suits willing to give, yet no one is asking.

Sometimes, I have so much money that I begin to send to people who have not even asked me. In such times, I am just waiting for someone to ask, but nobody does.

Don't ask someone with an abundance of shoes for a house, likewise don't ask someone with healing abilities for a car.

Know who to ask what from and you will not be disappointed.

When to ask

There is a time for everything. Even in asking for things, there is a time to do it.

Do not go to a man in pain to pile your problems on the person.

It is the wrong timing.

There is an appropriate time to ask people for things. If you get your timing wrong, it could spell disaster for something you could easily have gotten at the right time.

Most importantly, do not be an opportunist. Opportunists hardly contribute to the lives of people but go round taking from everybody.

If you want this principle to work for you, you must make the conscious effort to be valuable to other people so that in your time of asking, they can also look favourably upon you.

How to ask

To simplify the asking process, ask the right person: whether God or man. The right person is the one who has that which you need and is willing to give it.

Ask at the right time, there is an appropriate time to do everything.

Ask also for the right reasons. Don't go and ask for a car so you can drive your girlfriend around town.

Even the Bible has something to say about that:

Jas 4:3 Ye ask, and receive not, because ye ask amiss, that ye may consume it upon your lusts.

James 4:3

Let me end this chapter on this note.

One day I needed something seriously. I was in prayer and fasting to know how to get it.

Then, a name came into my mind. The man whose name came into my mind checked all the boxes I have outlined above.

He had what I needed, I had been of value to him on several occasions and I knew the right time to ask him.

Lo and behold, I did and he gave me that which I needed, he was smiling whiles giving it to me and it was a difficult thing to give. I didn't expect him to smile while doing it, but he smiled gladly.

Let us move deeper to master this subject and have the maximum benefit from it.

CHAPTER SEVEN:

THE ROLE OF PERSISTENCE

Persistence is a key trait for asking things into existence. The role of persistence cannot be overemphasized.

This is because, too many people give up when they are close to manifestation.

The Bible is clear about persistence when you are doing something good. There is the insistence to carry on as your reward will surely come.

Gal 6:9 Let us not become weary in doing good, for at the proper time we will reap a harvest if we do not give up.

Galatians 6:9 NIV

If we do not give up, the promise is that we will receive our due harvest. There is something about people who are persistent. They know what they want and are determined to get it. Neither do they stop till they get it.

You should be such a person, for it is persistent people who pull through to achieve the greatest things we see in our generation and generations to come.

These people do not give up so easily. They keep at it till they find what they are looking for.

Maybe this picture will help you to understand the reason you must not give up when asking or seeking things into existence.

Fig. 1 Giving up at the wrong time

Beloved, the word of God is true and it works. Do not give up on it. Stick to it and it will produce lasting results in your life.

Make the word of God the standard for your life. Make it the only truth you believe.

Those who give up too easily

The world is full of those who give up easily. They have become part of the numbers. A statistic.

That is not your portion. It is not your place. You must not be counted amongst that number. You are far above that number.

Those who give up easily are full of regrets. They wonder what would have been or achieved if they had kept on.

Just like the image, if the man finds out later in life how close he was to success, he might be devasted.

You see, why would you give up if the word of God has made it clear to you that what you are asking for or what you are seeking exists.

Rather than giving up, there are several other options one can explore. Among the options are a change of approach, or change of question or the recruitment of a team to help but never to give up.

Let me say this in passing. When looking for the picture above, I went to google and typed several things. I dd not get the picture but I knew the picture was available because I had seen it before.

After several minutes of searching, I still did not find it.

Did I give up? No. It is not in my nature to give up on something I know is available. I kept on searching but I changed my approach slightly and this helped me find the picture.

Those that give up easily do not accomplish that which they could have accomplished.

They do not find that which they could have found.

They do not reach where they could have reached, all because they gave up too easily.

Time will not permit me to include stories of people who never gave up and for that reason persisted to success.

These stories are all over history. Why not decide to be part of the success stories? There are people other than you that are looking up to you.

You are not doing this for yourself, you are doing it for the people who depend on you. You are doing it for generations unborn , who will read about you.

Like Paul, you need to persist despite the challenges and say:

2Ti 4:7 I have fought a good fight, I have finished my course, I have kept the faith:

2 Timothy 4:7

Such blessedness to read that statement. Despite the fact that Paul was beaten, arrested, shipwrecked, stoned, jailed and many other sufferings, he could confidently say he had finished his course.

Don't give up too easily, be a finisher. Else not finishing things will become a habit.

When it becomes a habit, that is a recipe for more failure in the future.

Team work

It is not always you can do things alone. Sometimes, you need to team up with another person or group of people to accomplish your task of seeking and manifesting certain things.

Personally, I have done it on several occasions. One that comes to mind immediately is when I needed to know how exactly to receive a vehicle to make life easier for me several years ago.

I had only one car and when it had a problem, I was stranded. I lived on a slightly isolated hill and without a vehicle it was difficult for me to move around.

I teamed up with a friend of mine and studied the word of God as well as other materials. We both came up with our own unique strategies based on what the word of God had said concerning provision.

We combined both of the knowledge we found and implemented it. Six months later, I had two cars. One more in addition to what I had. In that same period, my friend also had one car. One and a half years later he had two cars. In that same period, I got 4 cars.

We then knew we had finally found the key to settle the matter of vehicles. The word we found had worked.

We only have to fine tune it now to make the manifestation faster. The six months of application was nearly frustrating.

The joy though was overwhelming. To see the word work in such a powerful way was a thing of pleasure.

For years he struggled to get just one car. After applying the combined revelation we found, he got a car in six months.

Six months is better than all the years he went without revelation and without a vehicle. Team work works. It accelerates the seeking process.

See what the Bible says about teamwork:

Ecc 4:9 Two are better than one; because they have a good reward for their labour.

Ecclesiastes 4:9

A good reward for labour is what we all seek. Teamwork brings that into being.

Another great scripture about teamwork is below:

Mat 18:19 Again I say unto you, That if two of you shall agree on earth as touching any thing that they shall ask, it shall be done for them of my Father which is in heaven.

Matthew 18:19

If two work together in agreement, God intervenes based on the principles of teamwork and agreement.

Teamwork shortens the time of searching as well as the load and effort required. Perhaps it is time you gave your questions for manifestation to more people so that they can help you find the answers you need.

Personally, my first option would be to speak to a mentor. If mentors are not able to help, that is when I delve deeper into my own search into the Bible, books and other messages.

But like I said earlier, a team of people seeking the same thing makes the work easier.

Consider it sometimes.

Challenges

In every quest, there are challenges. These challenges come in different shapes and forms.

Some are devastating in their effect, some are mild.

Whichever way you look at it, challenges have a way of putting breaks to your momentum in whatever you are doing.

Nonetheless, there is something you must know about challenges:

They come to separate the boys from the men!

Imagine a world where everyone succeeded without any challenges. Everyone would be rich. Everyone would be successful

No one would like to work because they have money. Cleaners would clean no more. Judges will judge no more. Security officials will be relaxing in Bahamas.

There will be chaos in our system. That is why challenges are a very part of our ecosystem.

They come to stop those who really do not desire what they are looking for.

When you see a man or woman with a strong desire for something, they pursue it and get it regardless of the challenges that confront them.

I have come to love challenges. They are a sort of checkpoint to stop some people and allow others to pass.

Anytime you encounter a challenge, think of it that way. It is just a checkpoint to test your seriousness.

There are too many people who are not really serious about what they are seeking. They claim they are. They pretend they are but at the first sign of resistance, they run away.

This is sure proof that they were not even serious in the first place.

I remember when I embarked on my first 21 day fast of only water.

I had other people who said they will join me.

Within two days, they had all quit. I pressed on and completed it despite the challenges.

Challenges have a way of separating the serious from those that are not serious.

Desire

Strong desire helps in the pursuit of manifestation. That is the first thing I tell anyone who wants to succeed at an endeavour. Work on your desire.

Without desire, manifestation doesn't even come into play. See what the Bible says even about *answered prayer:*

Mar 11:24 Therefore I say unto you, What things soever ye desire, when ye pray, believe that ye receive them, and ye shall have them.

Mark 11:24

To even receive answers to your prayer, the starting point is desire. A strong desire does wonders. That hunger is a mark of every successful person.

Work on your desire. Feed it and grow it strong and you will accomplish so much that you never even dreamed of.

CHAPTER EIGHT:

THE ROLE OF FAITH

Faith is a common denominator in making the uncommon come to pass. It is a vital force in the life of every successful believer.

In our journey of asking things into existence, we need faith to achieve success.

For some of us, we have grown so much in our faith concerning certain things that there is no element of doubt we are dealing with in those areas.

We know the word of God works and have put it into practise so much so that we are rearing to go at any given time.

For others, their need for faith must be reiterated.

No matter the category you fall into, take your time and enjoy the words of wisdom in this chapter. It will bless you and increase your learning.

How can this be

This was the question Mary asked when she wanted to know how Jesus would manifest as a child seeing she was a virgin.

This was important to her because she wanted the words to come to pass but most importantly, to remove every doubt that could hinder the process.

The answer of the angel satisfied her question. That answer was the basis to determine whether her faith stood or not.

You see, as long as there is a revelation or piece of knowledge that you can base your faith on, the likelihood that you will not waver is high.

See the answer that was given to Mary:

Luk 1:34 Then said Mary unto the angel, How shall this be, seeing I know not a man?

Luk 1:35 And the angel answered and said unto her, The Holy Ghost shall come upon thee, and the power of the Highest shall overshadow thee: therefore also that holy thing which shall be born of thee shall be called the Son of God.

Luk 1:36 And, behold, thy cousin Elisabeth, she hath also conceived a son in her old age: and this is the sixth month with her, who was called barren.

Luke 1:35

The answer of the angel, coupled with the knowledge that Elizabeth had also achieved the impossible (she was pregnant though barren), assured Mary that she could now rest in full assurance of the manifestation of a son.

A son who would be the saviour of the world.

When you ask questions and you begin to seek and find the appropriate knowledge you need, something unique happens. The truth that you will receive that which you seek is no more in doubt.

That knowledge helps you to totally eliminate doubt. It is the evidence you needed to assure you that though you do not see the manifestation yet, you will have it.

This sums up what the scriptures talk about faith:

Heb 11:1 Now faith is the substance of things hoped for, the evidence of things not seen.

Hebrews 11:1

Glory to God, you have faith because you have evidence and this faith will cause the manifestation of that which is unseen because your faith is that powerful.

That is its realm of operation. If you doubt it, read this:

Heb 11:3 Through faith we understand that the worlds were framed by the word of God, so that things which are seen were not made of things which do appear.

Hebrews 11:3

The force which created the whole world was faith. You are operating such a force because of the knowledge you possess.

You are in good company.

This reminds me of this beautiful scripture:

Rom 8:28 And we know that all things work together for good to them that love God, to them who are the called according to his purpose.

Romans 8:28

You must go beyond believing and get to knowing that what you seek, you will find.

Let there be a knowing

Let us do a little illustration. Take your phone.

Look at it, what colour is it? Now that you have stated what colour it is, do you believe it is the colour or you know it is the colour.

Well, I guess you chose the latter. You know it is the colour. That is the point you must come to when it comes to your faith in the manifestations of the things you seek.

A knowing is a superior form of faith. I know my name; I do not have to believe it is my name. I know it is. When that happens, when you get to the point of knowing, there is no room for doubt or unbelief.

You ride on a certain frequency of confidence because nothing can hinder your faith at that level.

I pray that you experience that level of faith in every area of your life in Jesus name.

Let us see God operating in the knowing level of faith:

Jer 29:11 For I know the thoughts that I think toward you, saith the LORD, thoughts of peace, and not of evil, to give you an expected end.

Jeremiah 29:11

Beloved, understand that when there is a knowing, there is also an expected end. There are no two ways about that.

Your end is known and expected too. There will be no deviation nor disappointment whatsoever in Jesus name.

Do you know or do you believe? I pray you come to the point of knowing. It will take you to a powerful level.

Faith keeps you going

As long as your faith is intact, you will not relent in the pursuit of manifestation

Heb 10:35 Cast not away therefore your confidence, which hath great recompence of reward.

Once there is faith, the necessary steps for manifestation will be taken. The forces of heaven will be behind you and things will work to your advantage.

I remember this event vividly. A young man came to me wanting to go to the University. He had no money and his parents had little to give him.

I helped him ask the right questions, all along having faith that he will go to school. When it was time, he gathered resources from several places and embarked on his University journey.

He who had no money had made it there because a question triggered the necessary steps backed by faith.

Your faith will also take you places you never thought you will get to.

Your report shall be a good report. It shall be recorded in the annals of history. When a man or woman has faith, unwavering faith like Abraham, no matter how impossible to man the task looks, there is always the realisation that nothing is impossible with God, let that re-echo throughout your system:

Nothing is impossible with God

Dare to have faith till the end and your confidence will be rewarded just like Abraham, for the Bible says:

Rom 4:17 (As it is written, I have made thee a father of many nations,) before him whom he believed, even God, who quickeneth the dead, and calleth those things which be not as though they were.

Rom 4:18 Who against hope believed in hope, that he might become the father of many nations, according to that which was spoken, So shall thy seed be.

Rom 4:19 And being not weak in faith, he considered not his own body now dead, when he was about an hundred years old, neither yet the deadness of Sara's womb:

Rom 4:20 He staggered not at the promise of God through unbelief; but was strong in faith, giving glory to God;

Rom 4:21 And being fully persuaded that, what he had promised, he was able also to perform.

Romans 4:17

Beloved, keep the faith. Mighty things are performed by men and women of faith, yourself included.

This is not the time to waver. Once you can see the end clearly, you must just keep working towards it.

Needless to say, you will get there. It is written.

CHAPTER NINE:

PRINCIPLES TO MAKE YOUR ASKING(QUESTIONS) COME TO PASS

There are two basic methods we have seen to make our asking come to pass.

The simple asking and the asking of questions methods. Any of these can work for you, although many favour the asking of questions method because you gain valuable keys that can help you replicate that which you want manifested anytime you want.

When you are given the object of your desire because you used the simple asking method and you want a similar thing, you may be too shy to ask again. It is the nature of humans.

That is why the asking of questions method could be better. Nonetheless, my advice is to use both methods depending on the situation.

In this chapter, we will summarise both methods to make sure you can follow them and see manifestation.

Asking Method

This is the method that was adopted by Queen Esther. She needed deliverance for herself and the Jews. One man had the authority to grant it and so she had to ask that man.

This is what she went through to ask what she wanted into existence.

She determined what she wanted

What Esther wanted was the deliverance of the Jews. She determined it and set out to work towards it.

Many people do not get anything because they do not know what they want.

As long as you do not know what you want, it could be right in front of you and you will never get it.

Life has a way of doing that to people. The sufferings, routines, stress and business of life can make you even forget what you really want, even if the one who can give it to you is in front of you.

Learn to pause and determine what you want in life. The endless cycle of going nowhere isn't helping.

She knew who could give it

After determining what she wanted, Esther also knew who could give what she wanted.

In all the land they were in, it was only the King that could grant her request.

Many people make the mistake of asking the wrong person for what they want.

That is a mistake that is costly. It could be the difference between receiving your request or not. That is why it is important to know who is capable and also willing to give you what you want.

That might not be the case all the time but you must strive to ask people who qualify under these two categories; capable and willing.

Capable means they are able to give that which you want easily, willing means they are open to the idea of parting with that which you want.

Est 5:3 Then said the king unto her, What wilt thou, queen Esther? and what is thy request? it shall be even given thee to the half of the kingdom.

Esther 5:3

This is a typical case of getting anything you ask for from a capable and willing person.

Sometimes, God puts people your way that can help you and give you what you want, at other times, it is only God that can help you.

She prepared

Esther prepared herself in fasting before going to ask that which she wanted.

Battles are not won on the battlefield; they are won on the training ground.

You must prepare very well before you embark on asking. It could be the difference between receiving or not.

See another example of a man helping another:

2Ki 5:4 And one went in, and told his lord, saying, Thus and thus said the maid that is of the land of Israel.

2Ki 5:5 And the king of Syria said, Go to, go, and I will send a letter unto the king of Israel. And he departed, and took with him ten talents of silver, and six thousand pieces of gold, and ten changes of raiment.

2Ki 5:6 And he brought the letter to the king of Israel, saying, Now when this letter is come unto thee, behold, I have therewith sent Naaman my servant to thee, that thou mayest recover him of his leprosy.

2Ki 5:7 And it came to pass, when the king of Israel had read the letter, that he rent his clothes, and said, Am I God, to kill and to make alive, that this man doth send unto me to recover a man of his leprosy? wherefore consider, I pray you, and see how he seeketh a quarrel against me.

2Ki 5:8 And it was so, when Elisha the man of God had heard that the king of Israel had rent his clothes, that he sent to the king, saying, Wherefore hast thou rent thy clothes? let him come now to me, and he shall know that there is a prophet in Israel.

2 Kings 5:4-8

The lessons in this scripture are amazing. First of all, Naaman wanted to healed of leprosy. He knew what he wanted but he went to the wrong person for the solution.

Though the king of Israel could have been willing to help him, he was not capable.

This is what brought Elisha into the picture. Elisha gave him a direction which eventually led to his healing. Naaman was free because he had the help of a man who was capable and another who was willing.

Two people can thus help solve one thing. Sometimes you can ask a group of people instead of one person.

In the case of Hannah, she knew it was only the almighty God that could give her a child at that time.

This was simply because the priests were out of touch in those days.

She sought God earnestly and He came through for her.

1Sa 1:10 And she was in bitterness of soul, and prayed unto the LORD, and wept sore.

1Sa 1:11 And she vowed a vow, and said, O LORD of hosts, if thou wilt indeed look on the affliction of thine handmaid, and remember me, and not forget thine handmaid, but wilt give unto thine handmaid a man child, then I will give him unto the LORD all the days of his life, and there shall no razor come upon his head.

1 Samuel 1:10-11

Hannah sought the help of God and went into covenant with Him. Unsurprisingly she had a son, Samuel, who became a priest.

Ask in the right way and at the right time

When you know who to ask, the last thing to do before you receive is to gather boldness and ask.

But you should ask in the right way at the right time.

Do not ask for selfish reasons, ask for reasons that are worthy.

This will ensure you receive what you want when you ask.

The basic scriptural promise for this simple asking method is:

Ask, and it shall be given you

Matthew 7:7

Now that you understand how to go about it, let us go to the second method.

Asking Questions Method

This is the method used by the jailer, he wanted to know the way of salvation and he was told, paving the way for his salvation.

This is the process to use:

Ask the question the best way possible that will lead you to the right answer

The better the question you ask, the more likely you will get the right answer that can help you bring the things you ask into existence.

Many people do not ask questions and hence do receive get answers. Other people ask the wrong questions hence the answers they get do not push them towards where they want to go.

"What do I need to know to prosper?" is a far better question than "why are the witches of my family making me poor?"

That second question will not lead you to financial prosperity. I hope you get it.

Research every possible avenue to get the answer. (Persist till you get the answer)

After asking the question, you need to seek the answer.

You do this by research. Read your Bible, listen to messages, read articles, speak to mentors and any other avenue available to you to find the answer.

A take away point here is that, do not stop till you get the answer you need.

Take massive action on the answer.

Once you get the right answer, you need to put in massive effort to get the results you need.

Many people find the answers they need but put in very little effort in the answer or solution. This leads to miserable results, not because the answer was wrong but because the effort was lacking.

When the effort is right there shall be manifestation of the results that you desire.

For instance, If you find the answer to how to heal the sick, put in everything you have to manifest healing in the people you pray for.

The basic scriptural promise for this method is:

Seek, and ye shall find

Matthew 7:7

Now that you know what to do, do not wait any longer, choose one method and apply it now.

There are 30 questions I have prepared that will help you receive real transformation. It is in the next chapter.

Before that, please do well to get these courses. I did them for your benefit:

My desire is to see your progress and prosperity and freedom from negative people and circumstances. Because of that please permit me to introduce two courses that I believe passionately will help you.

1. To cure prayerlessness, an inconsistent prayer life and the pain of not enjoying all that God has made available to you because of the inability to have the prayer life you desire, click here to learn more about my 3 Day Course on How to Overcome prayerlessness that will solve the problem of prayerlessness in your life.

2.To overcome the pain of not having enough money to live where you want, eat what you want to eat and do what you want to do, I have created a 7 Day Financial Abundance Course that will deliver financial abundance to you quickly.

Click here to learn more about that course.

You will see increase and enlargement as you step out in faith.

Become a giant in your generation and beyond. It is well with you.

See next page

CHAPTER TEN:

30 QUESTIONS FOR TRANSFORMATION

In the next few pages, I have dedicated a question per page that will get you thinking, acting and changing directions as well as achieving certain things.

For every question, you can ask follow up questions that can help you better resolve the issues the questions bring out.

For instance, who is my mentor?

If you do not have a mentor, you can ask yourself why you don't have one.

Then you can ask how and where you can get one?

You can dedicate a day for each question so that you can do the follow up questions and get good time putting your life in order.

Get the next book in the series as you prepare to look at the questions.

Books In The Uncommon Results Series:

Book 1: Speaking Things Into Existence

Book 2: Asking Things Into Existence

Book 3: Praying Things Into Existence

QUESTION 1

What do I want in life?

QUESTION 2

What must I do to get what
I want in life?

QUESTION 3

What habits must I
eliminate?

QUESTION 4

What habits must I
develop?

QUESTION 5

How do I develop these
new habits and eliminate
the old?

QUESTION 6

What one thing can I do that will make all other things easier?

QUESTION 7

What can I do today that will make me feel accomplished?

QUESTION 8

Which books do I need to
buy and read this month?

QUESTION 9

Who are the people that
make me happy and how
do I reward them?

QUESTION 10

Who are the people that
stress me in life and how do
I make peace?

QUESTION 11

What is the most powerful

question I can ask today?

QUESTION 12

What can I do to make sure
my success is inevitable?

QUESTION 13

How can I prosper financially?

QUESTION 14

Where would I be in 5 years
if I keep doing what I am
doing?

QUESTION 15

What would I do today if it was my last day on earth?

QUESTION 16

Am I who I want to be?

QUESTION 17

Is my lifestyle healthy?

QUESTION 18

Am I preparing or prepared
for retirement?

QUESTION 19

How do I become a spiritual giant?

QUESTION 20

Am I spending time with the people I value the most?

QUESTION 21

Have I accomplished my dreams and goals?

QUESTION 22

What will I be remembered
for when I die?

QUESTION 23

Have I offered my life
everything I can offer it?

QUESTION 24

Why don't I do the things I should be doing?

QUESTION 25

What are my values in life?

QUESTION 26

Who is my mentor?

QUESTION 27

Who did I make better
today?

QUESTION 28

What important thing must
I do that I am
procrastinating?

QUESTION 29

What am I holding on to
that I need to let go off?

QUESTION 30

If not now, then when?

Thank you so much for reading this book. You are blessed and I love you deeply.

REVIEW

Because your review is important to help others benefit from these books, please leave a good review here

Please check out my other books on the next page

Other books by Francis Jonah

Other books by Francis Jonah

1. 3 Day Fasting Challenge: How to receive manifestation of answers

2. How to Have Outrageous Financial Abundance In No Time:Biblical Principles For Immediate And Overwhelming Financial Success

3. 5 Bible Promises, Prayers and Decrees That Will Give You The Best Year Ever: A book for Shaping Every Year Successfully plus devotional (Book Of Promises 1)

4. Influencing The Unseen Realm: How to Influence The Spirit Realm for Victory in The Physical Realm(Spiritual Success Books)

5. Prayer That Works: Taking Responsibility For Answered Prayer

6. Healing The Sick In Five Minutes:How Anyone Can Heal Any Sickness

7. The Financial Miracle Prayer

8. The Best Secret To Answered Prayer

9. The Believer's Authority(Authority Of The Believer,Power And Authority Of The Believer)

10. The Healing Miracle Prayer

11. I Shall Not Die: Secrets To Long Life And Overcoming The Fear of Death

12. Three Straightforward Steps To Outrageous Financial Abundance: Personal Finance (Finance Made Easy Book 1)

13. Prayers For Financial Miracles: And 3 Ways To Receive Answers Quickly

14. Book: 3 Point Blueprint For Building Strong Faith: Spiritual:Religious:Christian:Motivation al

15. How To Stop Sinning Effortlessly

16. The Power Of Faith-Filled Words

17. All Sin Is Paid For: An Eye Opening Book

18. Be Happy Now:No More Depression

19. The Ultimate Christian: How To Win In Every Life Situation: A book full of Revelations

20.Books:How To Be Free From Sicknesses And Diseases(Divine Health): Divine Health Scriptures

21. Multiply Your Personal Income In Less Than 30 Days

22. Ultimate Method To Memorize The
    Bible Quickly: (How To Learn Scripture
    Memorization)

23. Overcoming Emotional Abuse

24. Passing Exams The Easy Way: 90% and
    above in exams (Learning Simplified)

25. Books:Goal Setting For Those In A
    Hurry To Achieve Fast

26. Do Something Lest You Do Nothing

27. Financial Freedom:My Personal Blue-
    Print Made Easy For Men And Women

28. Why Men Go To Hell

29. Budgeting Tools And How My Budget
    Makes Me More Money

30. How To Raise Capital In 72 Hours:
    Quickly and Effectively Raise Capital
    Easily in Unconventional Ways (Finance
    Made Easy)

31. How To Love Unconditionally

32. Financial Independence: The Simple Path I Used To Wealth

33. Finding Happiness: The Story Of John Miller: A Christian Fiction

34. Finance Made Easy (2 Book Series)

FREE GIFT

Just to say Thank You for downloading my book, I'd like to give you these books for free.

Download these 4 powerful books today for free and give yourself a great future

Click Here Download

Your testimonies will abound. Click Here to see my other books. They have produced many testimonies and I want your testimony to be one too.

Made in the USA
Las Vegas, NV
30 November 2024

13024192R00125